CLASSIC FAIRY TALES

THUMBELINA

Retold by Jenny Nimmo
Illustrated by Phillida Gili

MACDONALD YOUNG BOOKS

First published in Great Britain in 1997
by Macdonald Young Books
61 Western Road
Hove
East Sussex BN3 1JD

Text copyright © Jenny Nimmo 1997
Illustrations copyright © Phillida Gili 1997

Designed by Shireen Nathoo Design

Typeset in 20pt Minion
Printed and bound in Belgium by Proost International Book Co.

British Library Cataloguing in Publication Data available.

ISBN: 0 7500 2021 0
ISBN: 0 7500 2022 9 (pb)

Once there was a widow who lived beside a river. She was poor but kind and longed for a child of her own. One day a beggar-woman came knocking at her door, and the widow took her in and shared a meal with her.

Before the beggar-woman left, she brought a small seed from her pocket. 'This is all I have to repay you,' she said, 'but if you plant it and water it every day, it will bring you happiness.'

So the widow planted the seed and watered it every day. At the end of a week a leaf appeared, then a long green stem crowned with a scarlet bud. One fine spring

morning, the petals flew apart and there, within the flower, was a tiny, tiny girl.

'I shall call you Thumbelina,' the widow said softly, 'for you are no bigger than my thumb.'

Thumbelina and the widow lived very happily together. Every day the tiny girl played on the kitchen table, singing in a beautiful clear voice. The swallows were returning from their winter home, and Thumbelina copied the sounds they made.

The widow made her a bed from half a walnut shell, with violets for a pillow and a rose petal to cover her. Thumbelina never grew too big for the little bed; she never grew at all, and the widow worried for her future. What will become of my tiny girl? she wondered. How will she survive in a land of giants?

One night, when Thumbelina was asleep, a frog jumped on to the window-sill; she came from the mud bank beside the river, and she was looking for a wife for her ugly son. Thumbelina seemed just right. The frog hopped over to the little girl, and gulped her into her big mouth.

'Help!' cried Thumbelina, waking up. But the widow was asleep and didn't hear her.

The frog carried Thumbelina into the river and set her on a lily pad. 'Now I shall go and make the house ready for you and my son,' she croaked, 'for soon you will be married.' Off she swam, taking no notice of Thumbelina's angry tears.

The fish in the river were sorry for
Thumbelina. They nibbled at the lily stalk
until dawn when the great leaf broke free and
carried Thumbelina downstream, safe from
the frog and her son.

A butterfly settled on the lily pad and
allowed the girl to throw her sash round
his head. His wings fanned out like white
sails and they sped along, faster
and faster.

'Life is going to be a grand adventure,'
sang Thumbelina, as she sailed down the
fast-flowing river but the next moment two
spiky arms grabbed her round the waist
and she was whisked away.

A stag beetle had seen her bobbing down the river and thought how pretty she looked. But when he called his mother and sisters to come and see his prize, they threw up their horny hands in disgust.

'She's human!' they shrieked. 'And so ugly.'

'Is she?' The stag beetle felt foolish. 'Shove off you hideous creature, he snapped at Thumbelina.

'I'm not hideous,' protested Thumbelina, and she ran deep into the woods where she hoped she would be safe. When night came she crept under a broad plantain leaf and fell asleep, exhausted by her extraordinary day.

All summer Thumbelina lived in the woods. She wove a grass hammock for a bed, and ate berries and tiny fragments of nuts that the squirrels left for her. But when winter came the woodland food froze and died. Snow began to fall and Thumbelina had nowhere to shelter. Cold and hungry she knew she must find another home.

At the edge of a field she came upon a little door set into a bank of corn stubble. Thumbelina knocked and the door was opened by a field mouse. When this good creature heard Thumbelina's tale of woe she said, 'You can stay with me all winter, but you must keep my house clean and sing to me every day, for I'm very fond of music.'

Thumbelina agreed and stepped into a room lit by twigs of luminous touchwood.

The tiny girl was warm and comfortable in the mouse's underground home. Her chores were not hard and she sang in her sweet clear voice as she worked. Sometimes

she could hear thumping and scraping beyond the door in the mouse's kitchen. One day the door flew open and there stood a creature, very smart in black velvet, but with over-large hands and tiny chinks for eyes, in a face that was otherwise all nose.

'Sir Mole!' exclaimed the field mouse, dropping a deep curtsy. 'What can we do for you?'

The mole had fallen in love with Thumbelina's singing and wanted to marry her. Would she come and inspect his wonderful home?

'You lucky girl,' whispered the field mouse, pushing Thumbelina through the door. 'Mole might be blind, but he is rich and clever.'

Not wishing to offend the two creatures, Thumbelina dutifully followed mole into his shadowy kingdom. This was nothing more than a maze of musty passages and Thumbelina's spirits sank. In one of the passages mole called out, 'Mind the dead bird. The wretched thing fell through my entrance.'

'Birds,' grumbled the mouse. 'They sing all summer and make no provision for the winter. Silly, carefree things.'

The bird was a swallow and when Thumbelina saw it, she was reminded of the birds that sang over her mother's house. She knelt beside it whispering, 'You are a poor bird, indeed, to die in such a gloomy place.'

In response there came a tiny heartbeat from beneath the bird's soft feathers. It was not quite dead.

'Hurry up, girl,' called the mouse. 'We're only halfway round.'

The mole took hours to show off his kingdom and Thumbelina was very weary by the end of the tour.

But that night she wove a beautiful coverlet of hay. When she had finished she took a twig of touchwood and crept into the mole's gloomy labyrinth. She found the swallow and laid the coverlet over him.

The following night Thumbelina took the bird a few grains of corn from the mouse's store cupboard. He opened his eyes and whispered, 'I know you, Thumbelina. I used to nest in the eaves of your mother's house. Thank you for saving my life.'

Thumbelina cared for the swallow all winter; the mouse and the mole never went near it for they couldn't stand birds. When spring came and the swallow was strong enough to fly, he begged, 'Come away with me, Thumbelina, for you don't belong down here in the dark.'

'I can't leave the field mouse, yet,' said Thumbelina. 'She has been good to me.' But when she saw the swallow fly into the sunshine, she longed to follow him.

The field mouse began to make plans for the wedding. She hired three spiders and three silkworms to spin silk and gossamer, and she made Thumbelina stitch and weave all summer long in preparation for the grand occasion.

The wedding day arrived. Dressed in shimmering white Thumbelina stood in the mouse's parlour. But she knew she couldn't

marry the mole. Somehow I must escape, she thought. 'I should like to see the sun, just once more before my wedding,' she said to the field mouse.

'Very well, but be quick,' snapped the mouse. 'Mole doesn't like to be kept waiting.'

Thumbelina rushed out into the field. Sunlight fell over the corn in bright golden waves, and the thought of a life spent underground was unbearable.

Just then, a swallow swooped over her head. 'Come with me,' he sang.

'Oh swallow I can't,' cried Thumbelina. 'Today I must marry the mole.'

'Mole will find another wife,' said the swallow. 'I will take you to the place where you belong.'

Thumbelina climbed on the swallow's back and he carried her halfway round the world until at last they reached a land of bright sunshine and unimaginable colour. The trees were a luxuriant green and the mountains white as marble, but best of all were the flowers that bloomed all year round, filling the land with their fragrance.

The swallow hovered close to a broad leaf and said, 'Step down Thumbelina. This is my winter home.'

Thumbelina slid on to the leaf. She was surrounded by tall flowers whose petals reminded her of something in her past. And then she became aware of a movement in the

centre of the flower beside her. A boy stood there, dressed in scarlet and exactly the same size as Thumbelina. Now she saw that every flower contained a tiny human being.

'I am a prince of this land,' said the boy. 'Welcome, stranger!'

'My name is Thumbelina.'

'Thumbelina doesn't suit you at all,' said the boy. 'I shall call you Maia.'

'Yes! Yes!' cried Thumbelina and then remembered who had given here the strange name.

'Will you tell my mother I am safe?' she called up to the swallow.

'To know that you are with your own kind will give her great joy,' sang the swallow. And away he flew, calling, 'I'll bring news of your mother next winter.'

And that is how Maia and her mother sent messages to each other across the world. But by the time Maia married the little prince, the swallow was too old to fly such distances, and his great-great-grandchild carried the story.

Other titles available in the Classic Fairy Tales series: